PHARAOHS

Stewart Ross

HODDER
Wayland

an imprint of Hodder Children's Books

ANCIENT EGYPT
Family Life
Food and Feasts
Pharaohs
Temples, Tombs and Pyramids

© 2001 White-Thomson Publishing Ltd

Produced for Hodder Wayland by
White-Thomson Publishing Ltd
2/3 St Andrew's Place
Lewes BN7 1UP

Editor: Liz Gogerly
Design: Stonecastle Graphics Ltd
Picture research: Shelley Noronha at
   Glass Onion Pictures
Consultant: Dr. J. Fletcher
Proofreader: Linda Crosby
Artwork: John Yates
Map artwork: Peter Bull

Published in Great Britain in 2001 by Hodder Wayland,
an imprint of Hodder Children's Books.
This paperback edition published in 2001.

Picture acknowledgements
The publisher would like to thank the following for their
kind permission to use their pictures:
AKG, London 7, 13, 22; **Art Archive** 4, 12, 14, 18, 26, 32,
40; **British Museum** (contents), 38; **Corbis Images** 9, 20,
23, 24, 27, 35, 36, 39, 42, 43; **Dennis Day** 41;
Werner Forman 5, 10, 11, 16, 19, 21, 28, 33, 34, 37, 45;
Hodder Wayland Picture Library 29; **Michael Holford**
(cover), 25.

Please note that the language of the quotations in this
book has been translated in a way to make it accessible to
younger readers. The precise date of each quotation is
generally not known.

British Library Cataloguing in Publication Data
Ross, Stewart
   Pharaohs. - (Ancient Egypt)
   1.Pharaohs - Juvenile literature 2.Egypt - Social life and
   customs - To 332 B.C. - Juvenile literature
   I.Title
   932

ISBN 0 7502 3537 3

Printed and bound in Hong Kong

Hodder Children's Books
A division of Hodder Headline Limited
338 Euston Road
London NW1 3BH

CONTENTS

1 The God-King Himself

'Bet it will!' said Madja fiercely.

'Won't!' said Seni. He was sure he was right. No one could build a pyramid that reached right up to the sun. Not even King Khufu.

'Will!' cried Madja. She pointed to the blocks of golden stone towering over the houses. 'Look, it's already as high as a mountain.'

Seni lifted a hand to shade his eyes from the morning sun. 'Rubbish! Just a little hill.'

'OK,' said Madja, 'I'll go and ask Dad.' She turned and trotted off down the dusty track that led to the pyramid.

Seni ran after her. 'Come back!' he yelled. 'You know children aren't allowed there. You'll be in serious trouble.' Madja ignored him. 'Listen,' he went on, jogging along beside her, 'I'm your brother and I'm older than you, so you have to do what I say.' Still Madja said nothing. 'I'm responsible for you, Mum said. If anything happens to you, I'll get the blame.'

Madja stopped and looked at him. 'Alright, if you're in charge, Seni, you'd better come too. To see I don't get into trouble.' She trotted off again.

Seni watched her for a moment, then turned towards their house. After a few metres he changed his mind. 'OK!' he called, hurrying back down the road. 'I'm coming! Wait for me!'

The most famous monument in the ancient world – King Khufu's Great Pyramid at Giza.

Amazement

After winding upwards for a while, the track turned sharp right and dipped down into a small valley. Rounding the bend, the children suddenly found themselves looking down on the entire pyramid construction site. They stopped and stared in amazement.

It was like a gigantic ants' nest. Everywhere they looked gangs of men were at work – on the pyramid itself, in the quarries, on the ramps, along the dozens of tracks, and in the masons' yards. Hammering, sawing, shouts of command and snatches of song floated up to the children on the hot morning air.

A carpenter at work. Unlike wealthy Egyptians, he is shown long-haired and unshaven.

'*For a long time King Khufu had dreamed of building a pyramid greater than any that had yet been built.*'

From *The Secrets of Thoth*, a story found on a papyrus document from about 1800 BC.

'What are you doing here?'

It was now Madja's turn to be afraid. 'Maybe we should go back,' she muttered. 'We'll never find Dad out there.'

Seni wasn't listening. He was already heading down the track towards the quarry. 'Come on, Madja!' he called over his shoulder.

When they reached the bottom of the slope, Seni led the way towards the masons' yards. Here teams of stonemasons were shaping the huge blocks of stone that had been cut from the nearby cliff. The children had not gone far before a supervisor spotted them. 'Oi! What are you kids doing here?' he yelled, striding towards them.

The king

When Seni explained who they were and why they were there, the supervisor relaxed. 'Well, your Dad's over there,' he smiled, pointing to a group of masons. 'Ask your question, then get out – before it's too late!'

Their father's face fell when he saw them. 'Oh my goodness!' he exclaimed. 'Of all the days to choose … ' A fanfare of trumpets sounded from somewhere near the harbour. 'Oh no!' he groaned. 'Kneel down and bow your heads. Now!'

Seni and Madja did as they were told. 'What is it?' whispered Madja, staring at the sand in front of her.

'Shh!' hissed their father. 'Don't speak! It's the king!'

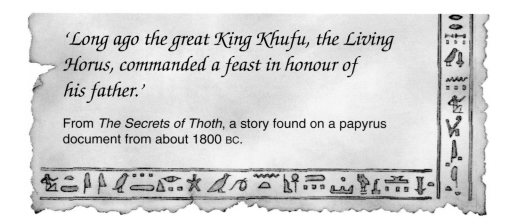

'Long ago the great King Khufu, the Living Horus, commanded a feast in honour of his father.'

From *The Secrets of Thoth*, a story found on a papyrus document from about 1800 BC.

'One day you will understand'

King Khufu was inspecting the work on his great pyramid. As the trumpets sounded nearer and nearer, Madja began trembling violently. She heard talking only a few metres away. A shadow darkened the ground before her. 'Child, why are you here?' a voice asked.

'I, I wanted to ask my Dad if the pyramid will reach the sun,' Madja stammered. The shadow disappeared.

After more talking, the shadow returned. 'Child, the Pyramid and the Sun will be one. One day you will understand.'

'The shadow went, the trumpets blared and the procession moved on. Stunned, frightened and confused, Madja and Seni walked home in silence. The god-king himself had given them their answer.

This is a tiny ivory statue of King Khufu, the Fourth Dynasty king who was worshipped for a thousand years after his death.

2 Lords of the River

The story of Madja, Seni and their father is set almost 4,500 years ago. The children and their father are imaginary, but Khufu was a real king who reigned from about 2589 to 2566 BC. We know little about him personally. But his pyramid survives as the Great Pyramid of Giza – one of the wonders of the world.

Originally encased in dazzling white limestone, the pyramid was a symbol of the sun-god. The king was son of the sun-god and the pyramid was his tomb. That is what Khufu meant when he said that 'the Pyramid and the Sun will be one'.

The land of the Nile

Our understanding of ancient Egypt must begin with the country's geography. Egypt is a land of barren desert and mountains. The exception is the strip of fertile land beside the River Nile, which flows from mountains in the south to a broad delta where it enters the Mediterranean Sea.

The river made the civilization of ancient Egypt possible. It provided water for drinking and for irrigating the fields. It was a 1000 km highway linking the kingdom's different regions. It provided fish for eating and mud for pottery and bricks. Papyrus reeds gathered from its banks were woven into household objects or beaten into an early type of paper (papyrus).

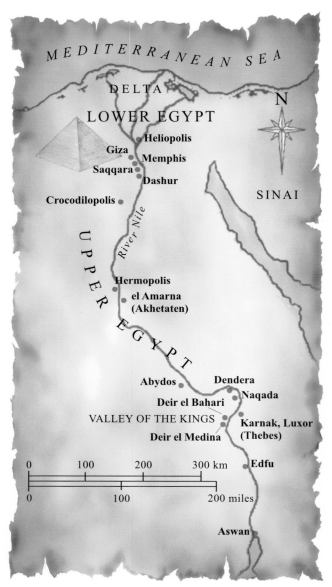

Ancient Egypt, the civilization of the River Nile.

The living waters

In the spring, the Nile ran low and drought threatened. Around June, it suddenly rose, flooding the fields along its banks. If the floods failed there was famine. When the river subsided, farmers marked out their fields and planted them with seed for a new harvest.

The Egyptians did not understand that the Nile depended on rainfall in the Southern Highlands of central Africa. The region was unknown to them. Instead, they believed the river was a living thing and worshipped it as a god called Hapi. They explained its cycles in the only way they knew – as religious events. The Nile's fall was a symbol of the death of the earth god Osiris. Its rise was his miraculous re-birth. Its floodwaters were controlled by the ram-headed god, Khnum.

The fertile strip on either side of the River Nile on which Egypt depended for its food.

'When you come into flood, you receive offerings, sacrifices of oxen and great praise.'

From a hymn to the Nile written for the Flood Festival at Thebes in about 1600 BC.

Horus-kings

Civilized life – settlements and agriculture – first appeared in Egypt around 5000 BC. Two separate cultures emerged, one in the north (Lower Egypt, nearer the Mediterranean) and another in the south (Upper Egypt, nearer the Sudan). By about 3400 BC, Upper Egypt's civilisation was overtaking that of Lower Egypt.

Upper Egypt had several towns, such as Naqada, Hierakonpolis and This. The kings of Upper Egypt, who were buried at Abydos, claimed to be related to Osiris' son, the sky god Horus. Horus' symbol was the falcon, the bird that soars over all. The names of these early kings, the Horus-kings, were always written beside the symbols for a falcon and a palace.

King Menes

In about 3100 BC Upper Egypt conquered Lower Egypt. Much later, Greek writers said King Menes was the first king of all Egypt and founder of the city of Memphis. Modern scholars are not sure that Menes even existed. They believe the conquest of Lower Egypt was carried out by King Narmer ('Baleful Catfish') or King Aha ('the Fighter').

Aha was the true founder of Memphis, the capital of Upper and Lower Egypt. After 2675 BC it replaced Abydos as the royal cemetery. By now Egypt was clearly a single country, ruled by kings who called themselves 'Lords of the Two Lands'.

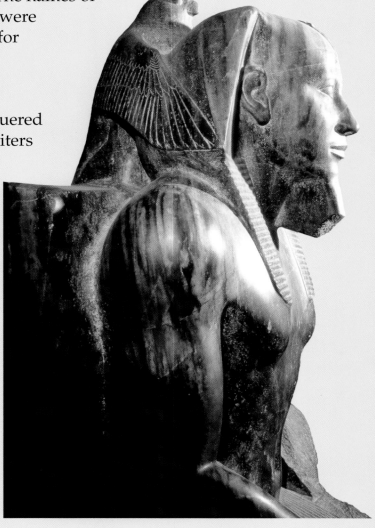

King Khafre (circa 2558–2532 BC), the builder of the second largest pyramid at Giza. His face is supposed to be that carved on the Great Sphinx.

A stone relief (carving) showing Horus and Hathor protecting two kings. One wears the Red Crown of Lower Egypt, the other the Double Crown of the Two Lands.

Kingship

It is almost impossible to exaggerate the importance of what the Egyptians had done. They had gathered together separate tribes and villages into two kingdoms, then united these into one huge country. There was nowhere else like it in the world.

At the heart of the Egyptian nation was the king. He had a capital city and a network of courtiers and civil servants to help him govern. But he was more than just a governor. He was, at least in those early days, a god. Sometimes he was referred to as *the* god, the Master of the Universe. No wonder Madja had trembled when King Khufu approached her!

'*Then Horus ruled the Two Lands as king, and all kings who came after him were known as the Living Horus.*'

From the story of *Osiris and Isis*.

Organize or die

How had Egypt's kings achieved such power? Much of the answer lies in the country's unusual geography. Because of the cycles of the Nile, the country depended on meticulous organization and co-operation.

During the flood time, for example, all the fields were under water. Food for this period had to be set aside and stored. Only a strong central government could manage this level of coordination.

Even more organization was needed when the waters went down. First, as much floodwater as possible had to be saved in basins and canals. This allowed irrigation to take place slowly. Second, as all the old field boundaries had been washed away, new ones had to be marked out. This meant records had to be kept and surveyors trained. The Egyptians called these surveyors 'rope-stretchers' because they measured out parcels of land with lengths of rope.

Rope-stretchers, storemen, record-keepers and other officials had to be fed and housed. To do this, taxes were raised from each household in the form of food and labour. This involved employing tax collectors and store-keepers.

If the system failed, Egypt would starve and its civilization collapse. That is why the king, who was at the head of the system, was so important.

A cross-legged scribe. The rare ability to read and write hieroglyphics made scribes very important members of society.

King-gods

Kings added to their power by linking themselves to gods. Horus was an obvious association. The king soared over his people in the same way as the falcon god soared over the earth – so kings had a special relationship with the god. That brought them closer to Horus' father, the earth god Osiris whose spirit guided the Nile.

Other ideas helped build up the king's god-like position. According to Egyptian teachers, order (or 'ma'at') was always under threat from chaos (or 'izfet'). The world was preserved from chaos by the gods, which was why it was important not to annoy them. Because the king was semi-divine, he could keep the gods on his side and so preserve order.

The king who restored his country's position in the world – Sety I, the vanquisher of Egypt's enemies, the Hittites. His status is emphasised by showing him as the god Osiris.

'He who rules over the Two Lands is a wise man.

From the *Wisdoms of Merikare*, a king of the Tenth Dynasty.

Pharaohs

So far we have referred to the rulers of Egypt as 'kings' and given them a single name. In fact, early kings had three names and later ones five. They all had a Horus-name, which linked them to the god. Other names associated them with the goddesses of Upper and Lower Egypt (the 'Two Ladies' name) and the sun god Re.

By about 1500 BC kings were also called 'pharaoh'. This is the name commonly (but wrongly) used for all Egyptian kings. Its origin is the word *per aa*, meaning 'great house' or royal palace. To avoid confusion, we will normally call all rulers simply 'king'.

King Ahmose, founder of the Eighteenth Dynasty and the New Kingdom. He is shown here being purified with holy water.

Gods or not?

Just how god-like were Egypt's rulers? The question is not easily answered because the king's status changed over time. Until about 2180 BC, however, all kings were seen as gods. They owned everything and were the soul of their country.

Then, after a troubled period, the kings' prestige was restored but some of their divine power was lost. It was more common now to see them as 'gods-in-waiting' – people who would be gods after their deaths. Finally, from 1069 BC onwards, the gap between how the kings saw themselves and how others saw them widened. Although many kings still claimed to be divine, most of their subjects were not so sure.

Dates and Dynasties

Much of the history of ancient Egypt is the history of its kings. They are the first individual people recorded in human history and their story runs more or less continuously from about 3150 to 30 BC.

During this period thirty-one families ruled Egypt in succession. Each family is known as a dynasty. Often, when a king had no successors his dynasty ended and a new one began. Khufu was the second king of the Fourth Dynasty (about 2613–2494 BC). The dynasties are sometimes defined with Roman numerals, so the Fourth Dynasty becomes 'Dynasty IV'.

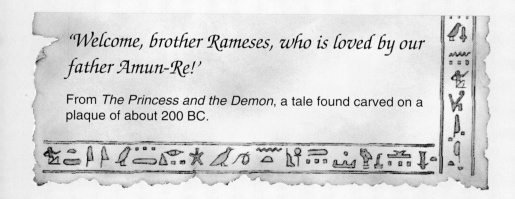

"Welcome, brother Rameses, who is loved by our father Amun-Re!'

From *The Princess and the Demon*, a tale found carved on a plaque of about 200 BC.

3 Kings and Dynasties

Ancient Egypt enjoyed three eras of greatness, known as 'Kingdoms'. Madja and Seni lived during the Old Kingdom (Third to Seventh Dynasties, about 2690–2180 BC). Then came a time of disorder – the First Intermediate Period. Egypt revived during the Middle Kingdom (Dynasties Eleven to Fourteen, about 2055–1650 BC) before a troubled Second Intermediate Period (about 1650–1550 BC).

The country flourished for the last time during the New Kingdom (Dynasties Eighteen to Twenty, about 1550–1070 BC). Finally, a chaotic Third Intermediate Period (about 1070–747 BC) led into gradual decline during the Late Period (Dynasties Twenty-five to Thirty, about 747–332 BC).

Remarkably life-like statues of the Fourth Dynasty Prince Rahotep, son of King Sneferu, and his wife Princess Nofret.

The Old Kingdom

The kings of ancient Egypt were at their mightiest during the Old Kingdom. They took on a new name, Sa-Re, which meant son of the sun god. The most impressive pyramids, huge symbols pointing to the home of the sun god, date from the Old Kingdom.

We have few specific facts from this period, but historians note certain trends. A king lived in his palace near his pyramid and left the day-to-day running of the government to his chief minister, the vizier. The kingdom was divided into forty-two regions, called 'nomes'. Each nome was managed by a 'nomarch'. Over time, these nomarchs became hereditary lords of their territories.

Breakdown

Three changes brought the glories of the Old Kingdom to an end. First, Egypt's climate was becoming drier. This reduced the grain harvest and made the country poorer. Second, the power of the nomarchs grew until some of them ruled their regions like little kings. Finally, King Pepy II (2288–2194 BC) ruled for so long that he became old and infirm and was seen as weak.

After the death of King Pepy II, the kings who ruled in Memphis lost control over the powerful nomarchs of the south. In about 2130 BC, the nomarch Akhtoy I actually founded his own Dynasty (the Ninth). The country was finally re-united by Montuhotep II (2008–1957 BC) of the Eleventh Dynasty. But it took a while for the Middle Kingdom to become established.

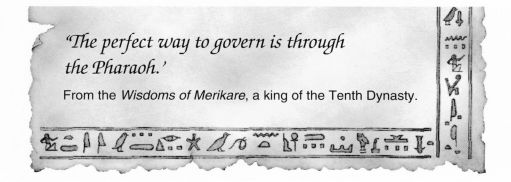

'The perfect way to govern is through the Pharaoh.'

From the *Wisdoms of Merikare*, a king of the Tenth Dynasty.

Amenemhet takes over

Montuhotep II and his successors of the Eleventh Dynasty were from the south of the country. Their government was based at Thebes, the ancient capital of Upper Egypt. The people of Lower Egypt felt neglected.

In about 1938 BC, Vizier Amenemhet, chief minister of King Montuhotep IV, rebelled against his royal master. Amenemhet overthrew Montuhotep and set himself up as king. The line of rulers he established – the Twelfth Dynasty – proved to be one of the most successful in Egypt's entire history.

One of the greatest of the great, King Montuhotep II who reunited the Two Kingdoms at the end of the twenty-first century BC.

Glories of the Middle Kingdom

Amenemhet I moved his government north and based it in a new city near Memphis. After his death, his son Senwosret I continued his father's good government.

The next five kings of the Twelfth Dynasty were able and lived a long time. They reduced the power of the nomarchs and took a close personal interest in the government. Egypt grew immensely rich through trade and many new building projects were undertaken.

Chaos again

The Twelfth Dynasty ended with the reign of Sobekneferu (1763–1759 BC), the sister and wife of Amenemhet IV. Brother-sister marriage was common in Egyptian royal families. However, woman rulers were more unusual, so Sobekneferu called herself 'king'.

During the reigns of the fifty-five kings of the Thirteenth Dynasty, who lived at Itj-Tawy in Lower Egypt, the kingdom again went into decline. The Nubians captured Egypt's forts in the south and foreigners came to settle in the rich lands of the north. Around 1675 BC, the country divided again. For a while two dynasties ruled, the Fourteenth Dynasty in the Nile delta and the Thirteenth Dynasty elsewhere.

Invasion and recovery

Around 1630 BC, invaders swept into northern Egypt from the east. The conquerors were the Hyksos. They set up their own dynasty of kings, the Fifteenth Dynasty. The old dynasties collapsed. Only in the south did Egyptian kings survive, but only just.

Egypt's recovery was started by King Seqenenre Tao. His son and successor, King Kamose (about 1543–1539 BC), defeated the Hyksos and their Nubian allies but died while still a young man. His brother Ahmose finally drove the Hyksos out of Egypt and brought the kingdom together under one rule. In honour of this achievement, the Egyptians declared him the founder of a new line of kings, the Eighteenth Dynasty.

Amenemhet IV, last king of the Twelfth Dynasty and ruler of a kingdom that was slipping into decline.

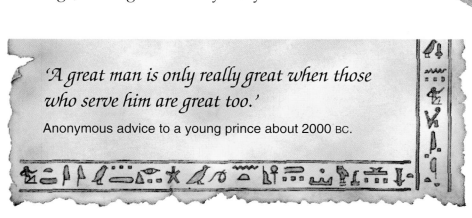

'A great man is only really great when those who serve him are great too.'

Anonymous advice to a young prince about 2000 BC.

The New Kingdom

The rulers of the Eighteenth Dynasty launched the New Kingdom period, when Egypt was richer and more powerful than ever before. Moreover, for the first time it became master of a huge empire. Stretching far beyond the kingdom's traditional borders, the empire changed Egypt from an inward-looking nation into an outward-looking one.

The conquests were begun by Amenhotep I, the son and successor of Ahmose. To remove the Nubian threat, he took his armies south to the third set of rapids on the Nile (the Third Cataract). This extended Egyptian rule much further into Africa than ever before. He also advanced north and east across Sinai, perhaps as far as the River Euphrates in Syria.

The Eighteenth Dynasty

The rulers of the Eighteenth Dynasty, whom we can now properly call pharaohs for the first time, were a fascinating lot. Amenhotep, whose only son died young, was succeeded by an army officer, Thutmose I. The line of kings he established lasted until the boy-king Tutankhamun died in 1322 BC.

The Thutmose line also included Hatshepsut, one of the greatest of the female pharaohs, and the brilliant Thutmose III – soldier, statesman, athlete and scholar. Other notable kings included Amenhotep III ('the Magnificent') and his unusual son Akhenaten. Married to the famously beautiful Nefertiti, Akhenaten

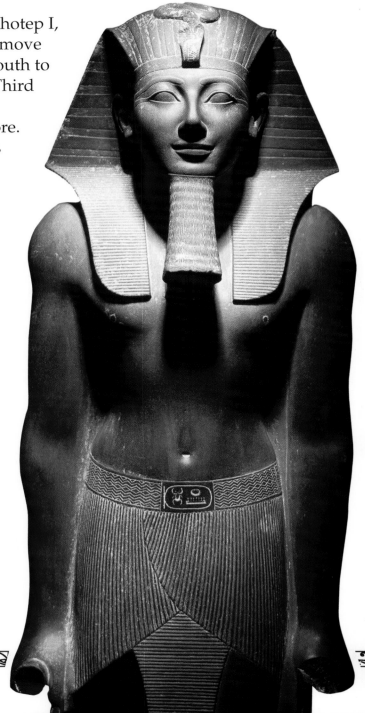

The warrior-king Thutmose III (circa 1479–1425 BC) who carved out Egypt's empire and constructed a series of striking monuments.

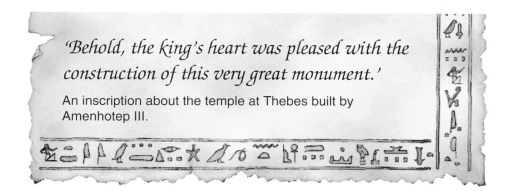

An inscription about the temple at Thebes built by Amenhotep III.

introduced a religious revolution by proclaiming Aten (the sun disc) as the god of gods.

The last of the great

Akhenaten's son was Tutankhamun. His death was followed by a scrabbling for power before a vizier, Rameses I, emerged as king in 1292 BC. He established the Nineteenth Dynasty. His son Sety I and grandson Rameses II ('the Great') ruled Egypt during its last period of true greatness. The foe in the north-east, the Hittites, were kept at bay, the economy flourished and huge building programmes were carried out.

After Rameses II's sixty-seven-year reign the tide against Egypt started to turn. Nubia rebelled in the south and 'Peoples from the Sea' attacked in the north. When the succession was disputed after the reign of Queen Tawosret, the dynasty ended in costly civil war.

A relief on the wall of the Great temple of Amun at Karnak showing King Sety I triumphing over the Libyans and Hittites.

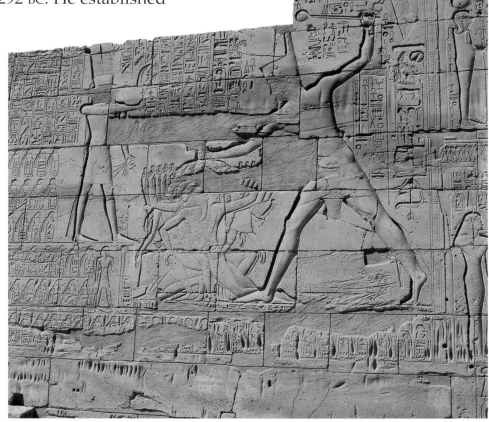

The glory fades

All the kings of the Twentieth Dynasty, apart from its founder Sethnakhte (1190–1187 BC), were called Rameses. Rameses III beat off attacks from Libya and 'Peoples from the Sea', and during the seventeen-year reign of Rameses IX Egypt was well governed. However, although the kings of the Twentieth Dynasty shared the same name as Rameses the Great, none of them matched him in glory.

The long reign of Rameses XI, the last of his dynasty, was a disaster. The king failed to deal with further attacks on the Delta region. Worse still, he allowed some of the priests and nobles of the Thebes region to become as rich and powerful as the king himself.

Dreaming of future glories? A relief of Rameses II (the Great) as a young man.

The beginning of the end

The Third Intermediate Period began with the death of Rameses XI and lasted for over 300 years. Five dynasties of kings came and went. The empire was lost. The country split first into two, then into smaller kingdoms. At times much of the land was under the control of the Libyans.

Surprisingly, it was the Kushites from Nubia who ended these centuries of turmoil. King Piankhy (747–716 BC) of the Twenty-fifth ('Kushite') Dynasty conquered the country and ordered all the lesser kings to accept him as the pharaoh. Although the Kushites tried hard to restore Egypt's former greatness, the world had changed. New powers and new civilizations were emerging that would soon eclipse Egypt for ever.

'The mighty pharaoh Rameses led his army to conquer vast territories and collect tribute from many cities.'

From the story *The Treasury of Rameses* told by the Greek historian Herodotus.

4 The Greatest of the Great

The kings and queens of ancient Egypt are shrouded in mystery. Most are scarcely more than names. Their grand monuments – the soaring pyramids and magnificent temples – tell us little about those who ordered their creation. Where we do have a written record, it is usually heavily biased. No king-god admitted making a mistake or being defeated.

Yet there are glimpses of humanity behind the mask of kingship. Amenemhet I's instructions to his son suggest a deeply cynical man. Realistic portraits of Senwosret III show a definite hardness. And the little statue of Akhenaten and his wife Nefertiti, holding hands side by side, is a touching memorial to their love.

Aha the founder

Of all the kings of the Old Kingdom, Aha was one of the most important. Although he is sometimes known as 'the Fighter', a more suitable name would be 'the Founder'. He was most likely the king who first united Upper and Lower Egypt into one kingdom, around 3100 BC. This is suggested in the 'nebty' name (*Men*) he took, honouring the 'Two Ladies' – the goddesses of north and south Egypt.

Aha founded temples to the gods, which helped him seem more divine. From his burial place at Abydos it is clear that he expected to move on to a glorious afterlife. To tend him there, several young servants were buried alongside him.

A life-like painted limestone statuette of Akhenaten and his famously beautiful wife Nefertiti.

The first king-god

Djoser, who ruled from about 2667 to 2648 BC, was known during his lifetime by his 'Horus name' Netjerykhet. Later generations called him Djoser (or Zoser) and honoured him as the first king who was also a god. This was enormously important. The religious authority that it gave the king helped him hold together and govern his large kingdom. Had he been just an ordinary person, these tasks would have been almost impossible.

Djoser also left the world's first stone monument building, the Step Pyramid at Saqqara. The difficulty of constructing such a huge and complicated building, in which the king was buried, shows how well organized Djoser's government was.

Montuhotep II

Montuhotep II (about 2008–1957 BC) reunited Egypt after the troubles of the First Intermediate Period. With Nubian help, he advanced gradually down the Nile from Thebes until he controlled the whole country. Interestingly, he changed his Horus name to match his success. Starting out as 'Hope for the Two Lands', he ended up as 'Uniter of the Two Lands'.

Montuhotep was a warrior and a tough ruler. But he does seem to have had a kind side to his personality.

The Step Pyramid at Saqqara, built by King Djoser in about 2650 BC. Over 60 metres tall, it was larger than any previous construction in the world.

Sharing his tomb are the mummified remains of his wives and close by are about sixty soldiers who had died fighting for him. He ordered their bodies to be buried next to him so they could share his life in the next world.

Senwosret and his grandson

Amenemhet I, the founder of the Twelfth Dynasty, was probably murdered in a plot involving his many wives. When his son Senwosret I (about 1965–1920 BC) heard of his father's death, he was fighting in Libya. He rushed home, seized the throne and went on to become one of Egypt's most famous king-gods.

As well as a soldier, Senwosret was a great builder. His White Kiosk (a shelter for the god Amun) at Karnak is reckoned to be ancient Egypt's most beautiful building. He and his talented grandson Senwosret II (about 1880–1874 BC) both founded new towns, Itj-tawy and Hotep-Senwosret.

Montuhotep II, the Eleventh Dynasty monarch who buried some of his soldiers beside his own tomb so they would share his immortality.

'You will live for millions of millions of years; a lifetime of millions.'

The god Atum's supposed reply to a king who asked how long he would live.

Women to the rescue

Women played a key part in setting up the Eighteenth Dynasty, the first dynasty of the New Kingdom. In about 1539 BC, the warrior king Kamose suddenly died while at war with the Hyksos invaders. His brother and heir, the ten-year-old Ahmose, was too young to rule and Egypt was once again threatened with chaos.

The situation was saved by Ahmose's mother, the formidable Queen Ahhotep, who ruled until her son was old enough to take over. Ahmose continued Kamose's work and drove the Hyskos right out of Egypt. He too was backed by a powerful woman – his sister-wife Queen Ahmose Nefertiry (about 1570–1505 BC). She worked so closely with her husband that she was the first queen to be given the special title 'God's Wife of Amun'.

Ahmose Nefertiry survived her husband, who died aged about thirty-five, and helped her son Amenhotep I (about 1525–1504 BC) get himself established. After a long and successful reign he was laid to rest in the same burial complex as his remarkable mother.

Hatshepsut and Thutmose

King Thutmose I (about 1504–1493 BC) had a daughter, Hatshepsut, and a son, Thutmose, by different wives. As was the custom, these two were married. When the king died, his son became King Thutmose II.

Queen Kiya, one of the lesser wives of King Akhenaten. She was probably the mother of Tutankhamun.

> *"The Mighty Horus, Lord of East and West of many years, Good Goddess, Holy Lady, Golden Falcon, King of Upper and Lower Egypt, Kamara, Daughter of Amon-Re, Hatshepsut.'*
>
> The full official name of Pharaoh Hatshepsut.

Hatshepsut bore a daughter. Her husband also had a son by a second wife. When Thutmose II died in about 1479 BC, his infant son became King Thutmose III. Then Hatshepsut took over. Somehow she got the child king out of the way, gave herself a Horus name and took over as pharaoh. She even wore the official false beard!

The reign of Pharaoh Hatshepsut (about 1473–1458 BC) was a time of peace and prosperity. Helped by her high official Senenmut, she ruled well and built several remarkable constructions. Her burial temple at Deir el Bahri is one of ancient Egypt's finest pieces of architecture. After her death, Thutmose III pursued a glittering career of his own.

The goddess Hathor on the columns in the temple of Hatshepsut (circa 1473–1458 BC), the most successful of Egypt's queens.

The heretic king

During his long, peaceful and prosperous reign, Amenhotep III hunted, got married several times, and supervised an enormous number of building projects. More unusual, he and his chief wife Tiy showed interest in a religion based on the god Aten.

Amenhotep the Magnificent died in about 1352 BC. For five years his son ruled as Amenhotep IV, then changed his name to Akhenaten, meaning 'Beneficial for the Aten'. The Aten was the disc of the sun – the king was following his father's religion to the exclusion of all other gods.

Akhenaten recognized just one supreme force – Light, which came each day through the sun disc. All the other gods – Amun, Re, Horus and so forth – were irrelevant.

Akhenaten was a poor administrator as well as a heretic. After his death, his son Tutankhamun restored the old religion. Later, most of Akhenaten's monuments were destroyed by Horemheb and Rameses II.

The great Rameses

King Sety I (about 1294–1279 BC) was an army officer before his father, Rameses I, established the Nineteenth Dynasty. Using his military experience, Sety waged successful campaigns against Egypt's most dangerous enemies, the Hittites.

Sety's son, Rameses II, is usually known as Rameses the Great. Egypt continued to flourish during his sixty-seven-year reign and future kings deliberately modelled themselves on him. Rameses kept the Hittites at bay and undertook massive building works. The grandeur of his temple in Western Thebes (the 'Ramesseum'), for example, remains impressive.

The head of Queen Nefertiti, probably carved and painted by the king's chief sculptor, Thutmose. She is remembered as one of the most talented and beautiful women of the ancient world.

However, our idea of Rameses is partly the result of his own image-making. He covered the land with huge statues of himself, often in the form of a god. Statues of him as Osiris, for instance, line the inside of his temple at Abu Simbel. He was, his scribes insisted, a great lover (father of 100 children) and outstanding soldier. Yet we know that his one battle with the Hittites, which he claimed as a great victory, was at best a draw.

The majestic temple of Rameses the Great in Western Thebes, which the Greeks called (wrongly) the Temple of Ozymandias.

'My name is Ozymandias, king of kings:
Look on my works, ye Mighty, and despair!'
Nothing beside remains ...

From the poem *Ozymandias* by the English romantic poet Percy Bysshe Shelley. He was inspired by a picture of a broken statue of Rameses the Great lying in the desert.

5 Empire

The doomed ones

The Egyptians were a proud people. They believed their civilization lay at the centre of the Earth and was the only one that mattered. As we have seen, their god-like kings were the proudest of all. Some of them, such as Amenhotep III, Khufu and Rameses II, probably believed they actually were gods. Everyone else – foreigners as well as Egyptians – was expected to respect and obey them.

This view of the world led Egyptians to hold all foreigners in contempt. They used words such as 'vile', 'doomed' and 'beyond respect' to describe them. A foreign leader was never called 'king' (only Egypt had a true king), but 'chief' or just 'big man'.

An isolated land

Egypt was cut off by geography as well as culture. To the west stretched the barren wastes of the Sahara Desert. The eastern frontier was guarded by arid mountains, the sea and the Sinai Desert. The Nubian Desert lay to the south and the Mediterranean to the north. It was not an easy country to invade and for centuries very few people tried.

Moreover, the Egyptians had little need for those who lived beyond their frontiers. They were self-sufficient in food and enjoyed the most advanced civilization of the time. The only reason for Egyptians to contact the outside world was to import certain rare luxuries.

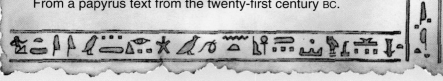

'*A person from Asia is like a crocodile on the river bank. He will grab at a single passer by but never dares attack near the city.*'

From a papyrus text from the twenty-first century BC.

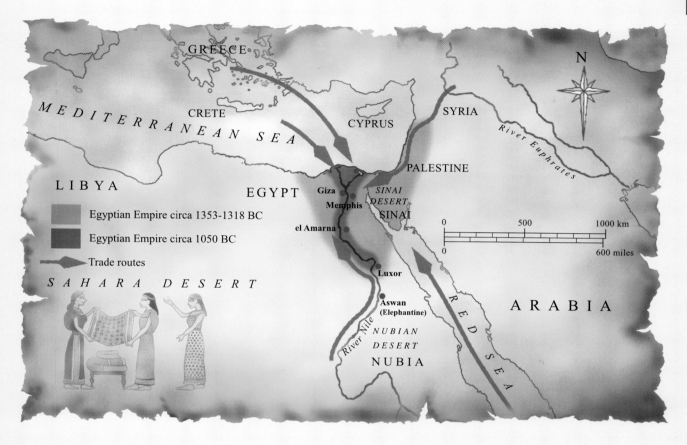

Northern Egypt, showing trade routes and the extent of the empire.

Tribute

Evidence suggests that goods were being exchanged between Egypt and western Asia before the reign of Aha. By the time of Madja and Seni, Egyptian grain was being widely traded for timber, spices, oil and other luxuries from ports on the eastern Mediterranean.

All trade was carried out in the king's name. Merchants were his servants and were not supposed to make a profit. There was no money in ancient Egypt. Strictly speaking, goods entering the country from abroad were not trade. Instead, they were described as tribute paid by foreigners to Egypt's king-god, lord-of-all. In the same way, Egypt's grain exports were called generous gifts from the lord-of-all to inferior people living beyond his kingdom.

Nubia

Only in the south did Egypt have continual contact with its neighbours over thousands of years. Above the first cataract, the Nile winds in a huge 'S' shape. The territory within and beyond the first loop is Nubia, the home of the Nubians and Kushites.

The name 'Nubia' may mean 'gold-land', which suggests why it interested the Egyptians. It was also a source of ivory, ebony, incense, exotic animal skins and slaves. For their part, the Nubians rarely lost an opportunity to raid north into the rich lands of Egypt. After centuries of fighting, the kings of the New Kingdom eventually conquered most of Nubia and built forts along the Nile to keep it under control.

Defence becomes attack

To the east and west of the Nile delta, the kings of the First Intermediate Period and the Middle Kingdom fought occasional campaigns against invaders. Then, at the beginning of the New Kingdom, the attitude of Egypt's kings towards their enemies began to change.

Libyan, Nubian and Syrian prisoners of Rameses III. Although he modelled himself on his great predecessor Rameses II, he was not so successful and at the end of his life he was threatened by a plot among his several wives.

Ahmose drove the Hyksos invaders from Egypt. His son, Amenhotep I, pursued them across the Suez peninsula and into western Asia as far as Syria. His successor, Thutmose I, continued these campaigns. By now the Egyptians were not fighting to defend their native land, but to conquer. Thus the Egyptian Empire came into being.

Fanciful victory – a painting on the side of a coffin shows the armies of Tutankhamun routing the Nubians. As far as we know, the king's armies did not fight the Nubians.

The Egyptian Empire

Thutmose III and Amenhotep II consolidated Egypt's gains in every direction. Their empire stretched from lower Nubia in the south, to Libya in the west and as far as the River Euphrates in the north. Although some of this territory was lost after Akhenaten, much of it was later recaptured by Horemheb, Sety I and Rameses the Great.

The warrior kings of the Eighteenth and Nineteenth Dynasties found that conquest brought them more than glory. Their new subjects, especially in the cities of the north, were rich. From Nubia, Libya, Palestine and Syria tribute of every kind flooded into Egypt. It was this wealth that funded the spectacular building programmes of Rameses II and others. For a time Egypt's king-gods really were lords of the Earth.

'Rameses the Great charged his chariot into the middle of the enemy and ground them into the dust.'

From the story *The Treasury of Rameses* told by the Greek historian Herodotus.

The kilt-wearers

Egyptian rule was toughest in Nubia. This was not
because the Egyptians had a lower opinion of the Nubians
than other people they conquered – the 'kilt-wearers' of
the south and the 'foul Asiatics' were both 'abominations
of Re'. Nubia was smaller and less densely populated than
the northern lands, so it was ruled directly by royal
viceroys (rulers sent from Egypt to control the area).

The viceroys demanded tribute in the form of precious
metals, slaves, rare woods and even ostrich feathers. Those
who refused to pay were said to be in rebellion. As a
punishment they could be transported to another part of
the empire. An even worse fate was suffered by those sent
to labour in the Nubian mines, where workers died like
flies in the scorching heat.

The Northern Empire

Syria and Palestine were harder to govern. Indeed, when
all the cities and states of the region allied, they could be
more powerful than the Egyptians. So they
were left to rule
themselves – as long as
they promised
obedience to the king
of Egypt and paid him
tribute. From time to time,
senior Egyptian army
officers called to settle
disputes and remind
everyone who was master.

Tribute from the north
included food, wine, wood (always in
short supply in Egypt), minerals and spices. It was sent to
Egypt at the taxpayers' expense. Sometimes local leaders
had to send their children to the Egyptian court. Here they
were held as hostages to discourage rebellion, and
educated in Egyptian ways.

Ancient cruelty – a Nubian
slave, bound by the neck,
is led off to captivity.
Slavery was an accepted
part of Egyptian life.

Legacy and collapse

The empire changed Egypt for ever. It made the country less inward-looking and brought it into closer contact with other peoples and cultures. Foreigners came to settle in Egypt, some at the invitation of the king. New words – and even new beliefs – entered the country. The phrase 'do business in Syrian', for example, came to mean almost the same as 'haggle' (to bargain and get the best price when buying goods).

The Egyptian Empire, like all empires, did not last. It had been created by energetic and ambitious kings. After Rameses II and Rameses III, the crown passed to a series of unremarkable men and in their feeble hands the conquests of their ancestors soon slipped away.

The triumphant Rameses the Great prepares to strike the heads of his enemies. The king lost no opportunity to make a public demonstration of his power.

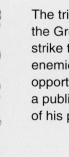

'I went on several Nubian-slaughtering expeditions, digging up their crops, chopping down trees and setting fire to their houses.'

Vizier Antefoker, who served Amenemhet I and Senwosret I.

6 Courts and Temples

The Residence

The king's palace was known simply as 'The Residence' because it was the only house in the whole kingdom that really mattered. King Khufu probably lived mostly in the palace beside the Great Pyramid he was building. Other kings had palaces at Memphis or elsewhere. Warrior kings built smaller palaces as campaign headquarters near where they were fighting.

The main evidence for what royal palaces looked like comes from the New Kingdom. The principal rooms, decorated with bright tiles and paintings, were a magnificent throne room and an airy courtyard with columns round the outside. The king made public appearances from a balcony in the outside wall known as the 'window of appearances'.

A silver Horus collar found in the tomb of Tutankhamun. Wealthy Egyptians of both sexes wore extravagant jewellery.

The heart of Egypt

The king-god was everything to Egypt – chief priest, president and army commander all rolled into one. In fact, king is not really an accurate translation of his role. The Egyptians knew him by several titles, including pharaoh, *Nyswt* (governor) or just *hm* (his majesty).

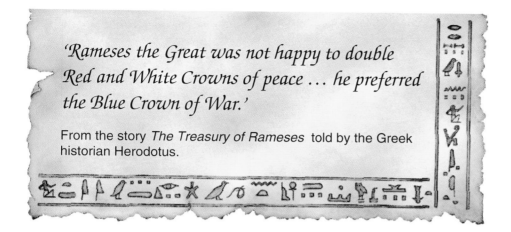

'Rameses the Great was not happy to double Red and White Crowns of peace ... he preferred the Blue Crown of War.'

From the story *The Treasury of Rameses* told by the Greek historian Herodotus.

The royal palace, therefore, was the administrative, religious and military heart of Egypt. It was like a small village, with kitchens and stores as well as bedrooms, reception rooms and bathrooms for the king and his family, courtiers, generals, viziers and priests. The king had to control this army of helpers. If they got too powerful, as happened at the end of the Twelfth Dynasty, they threatened his power.

At peace in the garden – Tutankhamun and Queen Ankhesenamun, the third daughter of Nefertiti. She is shown wearing a cone of perfumed oil on her head.

Clothing and symbols

A king's clothes were deeply significant. He wore a formal wig and false beard. As the gods had beards, so the king-gods had to have them too – even the women. Kings are shown in the white robes of a priest and in everyday dress: bare-chested with a white kilt and a striped head-dress of blue and gold. In formal pictures they hold a crook and flail, emblems of royalty.

Egyptian crowns were made of many materials, including cloth. The most important were the Red Crown of Lower Egypt and the White Crown of Upper Egypt. When worn together – symbolizing the Lord of the Two Lands – they made the Double Crown. A rearing cobra over the forehead symbolized the goddess and protector of Egypt.

The king-priest

Egyptian religion involved rituals – repeating significant acts to please the gods. Such rituals ranged from the offering of food to a god each morning to an annual procession in their honour. The day-to-day rituals were carried out by priests. But because the king was the chief priest, on special occasions he led the ceremonies.

The picture below shows Rameses III in the temple at Heliopolis. Carrying the crook and flail, he is wearing the white robe of a priest and the Red Crown of Lower Egypt. Before him are the gods and goddesses: Re-Harakhte (sun god), Atum (Creator), Iusaas (local goddess) and Hathor (goddess of love and beauty).

Coronation

The most important ceremony in a king's life was his coronation. It was of supreme importance for Egypt, too: the moment when a man became Horus (the sky god and, in later mythology, the son of Osiris and Isis). The coronation gave the people of Egypt a god to guide and protect them.

The long ceremony was full of complicated rituals. The throne represented the goddess Isis (Horus' mother).

Rameses III in the temple at Heliopolis. Kings were chief priests as well as rulers and army commanders.

When the uncrowned king sat on the throne, he sat in the goddess' womb. His rising from the throne – leaving the womb – represented his birth as Horus. Then a flock of birds was released to carry the good news to every corner of the Earth.

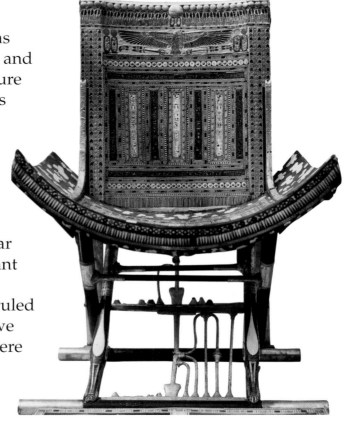

One of Tutankhamun's ceremonial chairs from the Eighteenth Dynasty, made of ebony and ivory and decorated with precious stones and gold inlay.

The Royal Family

Like her husband, an Egyptian queen was divine. She was the queen-goddess, wife and often sister of the king-god. We are not sure why kings married their sisters – perhaps it was to keep the bloodline pure. It could also have been to emphasise their divinity – gods and goddesses did not have to follow the same rules as ordinary mortals.

On ceremonial occasions kings and queens appeared together wearing similar crowns. Many queens played an important part in government, too. Some, like Hatshepsut, ruled on their own. Others ruled on behalf of their young sons. As far as we know, the children of a royal marriage were well treated – it was not wise to annoy someone who might become a god or goddess one day.

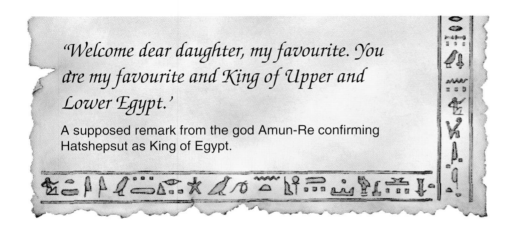

"Welcome dear daughter, my favourite. You are my favourite and King of Upper and Lower Egypt.'

A supposed remark from the god Amun-Re confirming Hatshepsut as King of Egypt.

Graves and robbers

King Khufu was eventually buried inside the Great Pyramid that he had built. The pyramid was his tomb, his monument and his path to eternal life. To us it seems odd, even gloomy, that a man should spend so much of his life thinking about his death. But Khufu did not see it like that. For him death was just a doorway to a better life with the gods. His tomb was a 'house of eternity'.

Interestingly, even in Egyptian times many royal tombs were robbed of their valuable contents. This suggests that belief in the king-god was not as widely held as the kings themselves would have liked.

The Valley of the Kings

When a king died, he ceased to be Horus in human form – that honour passed to his successor. Instead, he became mystically part of Horus' father, Osiris. This applied to the female pharaohs too, such as Hatshepsut. A king's final resting place – pyramid or tomb – was therefore a place of worship. For this purpose, special temples were built nearby.

During the New Kingdom, kings were buried in tombs carved out of the sheer rock of a dried-up river bed. This is now known as the Valley of the Kings. It has an amazing network of tunnels, staircases, shafts and storerooms. The burial chambers themselves are carved or painted with a glorious collection of spells, histories and images.

Eternal Memory

During the Old Kingdom, a king's tomb and burial temple (where he could be worshipped after his death) were on the same site. This had changed by the New Kingdom. Hatshepsut and

Cool rule – a highly decorated fan found in the tomb of King Tutankhamun. It was once set with ostrich feathers.

> *'Raise yourself, O king! You have not died!'*
>
> A common command found in pyramid texts left in the tombs of mummified kings.
>
> *'The king sent me to Elephantine to bring a granite door and lintels for the upper chamber of the pyramid.'*
>
> From the *Inscription of Weni* at Abydos, telling the story of a successful nobleman of the Sixth Dynasty.

Rameses II, for example, were buried in the Valley of the Kings. But to put off tomb raiders their temples were built some distance away.

These temples are some of the finest monuments in all ancient Egypt. Rameses' temple – the 'Ramesseum' – is as bold, huge and confident as its builder. Hatshepsut's, perhaps like the queen herself, is elegant, stylish and altogether more gentle. They survive, as was intended, to keep alive the memory of remarkable rulers of an equally remarkable civilization.

Hatshepsut's burial temple at Deir el Bahri.

7 Uncovering Ancient Egypt

The Late Period of ancient Egyptian history was marked by many invasions. The Kushite Dynasty was attacked by the warlike Assyrians. After a period of recovery under the Egyptian kings of the Twenty-sixth Dynasty, the land fell to Persian invaders. When Alexander the Great conquered the country in 332 BC, the long era of Egyptian greatness was finally over.

By Roman times, most of Egypt's monuments had become neglected symbols of a bygone age. Centuries later, the Renaissance sparked new interest in the ancient world. Since the discovery of the Rosetta Stone following the French conquest of Egypt, the world's fascination with ancient Egypt has continued undiminished to this day.

Robbers and historians

Many Egyptian tombs and other monuments were robbed even in ancient times. Nineteenth-century collectors continued the process, sending back hundreds of Egyptian works of art to Europe and the United States. Fortunately, serious investigation by archaeologists eventually replaced

The beginning of a modern industry – Victorian tourists inspect the ruins at Karnak in about 1865.

this insensitive plundering. The most exciting achievement of the early archaeologists was Howard Carter's discovery of Tutankhamun's largely unspoilt tomb in the Valley of the Kings in 1922.

During the 1960s a huge dam was constructed across the Nile at Aswan. While it was being built, archaeologists and engineers from several countries examined – and even moved – the many valuable monuments that would eventually be flooded by the new lake behind the dam. More recently, Egypt's growing tourist industry has boosted interest in the country's spectacular past.

The Egyptian legacy

Our division of time into hours, days and months comes from ancient Egypt. Its astronomers devised a calendar of 365 days, divided into twelve equal months of 30 days, with five spare days. They also used the twenty-four-hour day, and invented the water clock – the world's first timepiece – to measure the passing of time.

Greek builders borrowed the Egyptian design of lofty stone columns. This style of architecture was adopted by the Romans and, since the Renaissance, has spread world-wide. Modern medicine originated in the Egyptian port of Alexandria. Christianity, too, owes a debt to the ancient Egyptians – early images of the Virgin Mary and the infant Jesus are very like those of Isis and Horus.

Tutankhamun riding on a leopard – just one of the many elegant and beautiful treasures found in his tomb.

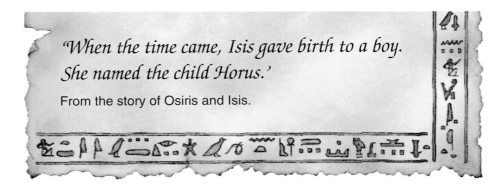

'When the time came, Isis gave birth to a boy. She named the child Horus.'

From the story of Osiris and Isis.

Primary sources

Our information about Egypt comes from two main groups of sources: archaeology and writing. Egyptian writing changed over the centuries. For a long time they used a language written down as hieroglyphs. These were carved on stone or written on pieces of papyrus. Hundreds of papyrus fragments remain, but they are very fragile. They are not easy to understand, either. For example, the same basic sign is used for 'canal' and 'love'!

Archaeological remains range from fragments of pottery to giant pyramids. Fortunately, the Egyptians built in brick and long-lasting stone. These materials have survived well in the hot, dry climate. The custom of burying everyday objects with the bodies of their owners also helps. An undisturbed Egyptian grave is like a fascinating time capsule.

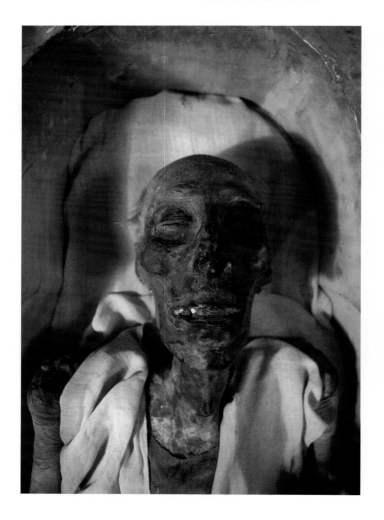

Ghostly glory – the mummified face of Rameses the Great.

The eternal mystery

We will never fully understand the civilization of ancient Egypt. Too much evidence has been lost. We are left with tantalizing clues, but these are only a few of the stones that make the huge mosaic. We have to imagine the rest of the picture.

The Egyptians recorded *how long* a king reigned, for example, but not *when*. They kept no continuous count of the years. More confusing, our years and theirs are not the same. They based theirs on the cycles of the moon, not (as we do) on orbits of the Earth round the Sun. The best we can do is estimate dates from their references to the position of Sirius, the Dog Star.

The Rosetta Stone

Nevertheless, our knowledge about ancient Egypt has grown considerably over the last two hundred years. The most important advance began in 1799, when one of Napoleon's officers found an odd-shaped stone in Rosetta (Rashid), near Alexandria. It was carved with Greek, hieroglyphic and demotic (a later type of Egyptian writing) letters.

A Frenchman, Jean-François Champollion, discovered that the three types of writing were different versions of the same text. The hieroglyphs, he realized, were a translation of the Greek. As he understood Greek, he was able to work out the meaning of the hieroglyphs. Finally, after centuries of mystery, historians were able to read the language of ancient Egypt and understand more of its long-lost secrets.

'To set up in the most prominent place of every temple an image of the ever-living King Ptolemy.'

From the Rosetta Stone, which describes how a shrine was to be set up in honour of King Ptolemy V.

Hieroglyphs, like these on the inside of a coffin of the fourth century BC, remained a mystery until deciphered by scholars in 1820. This extract is from the *Book of the Dead*.

Glossary

Archaeologist
Someone who studies the past by examining physical remains, usually through excavation.

Assassination
Murder of an important political figure.

Cataracts
Rapids.

Complex
Group of buildings.

Courtier
Someone who attends the royal court.

Crook
Shepherd's pole with a loop on the end for catching sheep by the leg.

Deity
God or goddess.

Delta
Where a river spreads into several channels as it nears the sea.

Divine
Of a god or goddess.

Drought
Time of no rainfall and severe water shortage.

Dynasty
Ruling family.

Ebony
Hard, dark wood.

Eternity
For ever and ever.

Exports
Goods sold to another country.

Flail
Stick for threshing corn.

Empire
Several lands under the rule of an emperor or empress.

Famine
A time of food shortage.

Hereditary
Passing on from one generation to the next.

Hieroglyph
Ancient Egyptian form of writing that used symbols rather than an alphabet.

Hittites
People who invaded the Middle East in the fourteenth century BC.

Hyksos
People who invaded Egypt in the seventeenth century BC.

Imports
Goods brought into a country from abroad.

Incense
Mixture that gives off a pleasant smell when burned.

Inscription
Short piece of writing, carved in stone or wood.

Kush
Area in western Nubia.

Lower Egypt
Northern Egypt.

Nome
Province.

Nomarch
Royal officer in charge of a nome.

Nubia
The region of northern Sudan.

Papyrus
Tough river reed. The Egyptians made its stems into a type of paper, also called papyrus.

Pharaoh
Originally the king's 'great house'. Later, it was used to mean the person from the great house – the king himself.

Renaissance
Development of arts in Western Europe, from the late fourteenth century onwards, associated with renewed interest in ancient Greece, Egypt and Rome.

Ritual
Important or significant action done regularly over and over again.

Scribe
Someone skilled at writing.

Stonemason
Someone who cuts and carves stone.

Surveyor
Someone who examines carefully a piece of land.

Upper Egypt
Southern Egypt.

Vizier
Important adviser and minister in the king's household.

Time Line

All dates are BC and approximate only.

7000–5500	Neolithic Age.
5500–3150	Pre dynastic Period. Badarians settle in Upper Egypt. Hieroglyphic writing begins.
3150–2690	Archaic Period (Dynasties 1 & 2).
2690–2180	Old Kingdom (Dynasties 3–6). Sphinx and Great Pyramid at Giza built. Wars against Nubians and Libyans.
2180–2055	First Intermediate Period (Dynasties 7–10).
2055–1650	Middle Kingdom (Dynasties 11–14). King Mentuhotep reunites Egypt.
1650–1550	Second Intermediate Period (Dynasties 15–17). Horses introduced. Bronze used.
1550–1070	New Kingdom (Dynasties 18–20). Reigns of Hatshepsut, Thutmose III and Tutankhamun. Tombs built in the Valley of the Kings. Temple of Amenhotep III built at Luxor. Reigns of Rameses II and III.
1070–747	Third Intermediate Period (Dynasties 21–24). Conquest by Nubians.
747–332	Late Period (Dynasties 25–30). Conquest by Assyrians and Persians.
332–305	Conquest by Alexander the Great. Ptolemaic Dynasty.

Further Information

Books for children:
An Ancient Egyptian Child by J. Fletcher (Working White, 1999)
Ancient Egypt by K. Hayden (World Books, 1998)
People Who Made History in Ancient Egypt by J. Shuter (Hodder Wayland, 2000)
The Ancient Egyptians by J. Shuter (Hodder Wayland, 1998)
The Awesome Egyptians by T. Deary (Scholastic, 1997)

Books for older readers:
Ancient Egypt edited by D. Silverman (Duncan Baird, 1997)
Everyday Life in Egypt in the Days of Rameses the Great by P. Montet (University of Pennsylvania, 1998)
The British Museum of Ancient Egypt by S. Quirke and J. Spencer (Thames and Hudson, 1996)
The Egyptians by C. Aldred (Thames and Hudson, 1998)

Internet sites:
Browse with care! While there are some excellent sites on ancient Egypt, there are also some inaccurate ones. You may like to start with these.
http://www.guardians.net/egypt
http://www.sptimes.com/egyptcredit.4.html
http://www.clpgh.org/cmnh/exhibits/egypt
http://www.ancientegypt.co.uk/menu.html

Places to visit:
The British Museum in London, UK, the Metropolitan Museum in New York, USA and the Cairo Museum in Cairo, Egypt, have excellent exhibits on ancient Egypt. Of course, a visit to the many sites in Egypt itself will give you a wonderful insight into that country's spectacular past.

Index

Numbers in **bold** refer to pictures.